BOTTLING
FOG

BOTTLING
FOG

ESSENTIAL LESSONS
IN LEADERSHIP

JOSEPH F. MURPHY

TEACHERS COLLEGE PRESS

TEACHERS COLLEGE | COLUMBIA UNIVERSITY

NEW YORK AND LONDON

Published by Teachers College Press®, 1234 Amsterdam Avenue, New York, NY 10027

Copyright © 2020 by Teachers College, Columbia University

Cover photo courtesy of Erik Sorenson via a Creative Commons license.

Library of Congress Cataloging-in-Publication Data

Names: Murphy, Joseph, 1949– author.
Title: Bottling fog : essential lessons in leadership / Joseph Murphy.
Description: New York, NY : Teachers College Press, 2020.
Identifiers: LCCN 2020023667 (print) | LCCN 2020023668 (ebook) | ISBN 9780807764428 (paperback) | ISBN 9780807764435 (hardcover) | ISBN 9780807779118 (ebook)
Subjects: LCSH: Educational leadership.
Classification: LCC LB2806 .M856 2020 (print) | LCC LB2806 (ebook) | DDC
    371.2/011—dc23
LC record available at https://lccn.loc.gov/2020023667
LC ebook record available at https://lccn.loc.gov/2020023668

ISBN 978-0-8077-6442-8 (paper)
ISBN 978-0-8077-6443-5 (hardcover)
ISBN 978-0-8077-7911-8 (ebook)

Printed on acid-free paper
Manufactured in the United States of America

Introduction

The Lesson of Positive Leadership

Bottling Fog is the culmination of 50 years' work to capture the core ingredients of leadership. The lessons come from reading, seeing, and hearing about leadership in various sectors of practice. I think about this as unpacking of the nucleus of leadership and presenting it in a way that we rarely see—pulling the fog into meaningful forms other than textbooks, lectures, or films, in other words, lessons. Each lesson is presented in a simple manner. But each presents a profound slice of understanding for leaders. Lessons are crafted in a way that they will not get lost as a leader walks to their car at the end of the day.

Each leader will already have lessons wired into their life and work. Looking into the bottle will show leaders important understandings that could be helpful.

For example, we see this lesson in the bottle: Good leadership rests upon assets and unfolds in positive ways. Poor leadership rests upon deficit pillars and unfolds in terms of inadequacies and failures. It does not require a guru or academic star to see this reality on a routine basis in schools—in classrooms, meetings, and other public spaces. Many of the negative actions that one hears or observes hurt other people, damage the organization, and cripple leadership and teaching. If change is desired, 5 minutes of reflection every night for 2 weeks will help one see the unobserved normal. Errors and poor moves will not need to be mined from distant and deep academic caves. Wisdom will stand directly in front of leaders (e.g., administrators, teachers, and staff) who can help the system improve without securing another degree or completing 3 days of professional development.

Effective leaders do not pound on people for errors. They help people learn how to perform appropriately, to spur development. They tell themselves before bedtime that they will talk

1

with (and not tell) Mrs. L., Ms. R., and Mr. E. tomorrow in a way that each absorbs recognition and respect to improve. They will converse with each individual in a manner that promotes specific growth and avoids damage and stagnation. What did Mrs. L. do well? How can I acknowledge that in an authentic, meaningful, and relevant way? (Leadership requires me to open, not close, doors.) But how can I help Mrs. L. not only absorb recognition and respect, but also wrap that around an understanding of the need to do even better? Such a conversation could unfold as follows :

> You know, Mrs. L., your students not only look happier in the cafeteria, but they also tell me that they are happier. And when I spoke with Corbette about why that is, the case is that she told me that she knows you really like her. Two months ago, I would have heard a very different answer. I just want to let you know how special this is. It made my entire day light up. Oh here, I almost forgot, Mrs. L. [hands Mrs. L. a buckeye]—grab this. I found it on my walk last evening. It's a buckeye, and they bring good luck. I have one here on my desk and one at home.
>
> I was watching Peter and Marcus yesterday. When I spoke with them before then, they really felt like they had no other friends. So I started thinking of all the great work you have done bringing happiness and friendship to them. I wonder if I can link up with you and do the same thing for them. I'll go to work at the school level. You go to work in your classroom. I'll have your back and we can decide the things we can do and the ways I can support you. What do you think?
>
> Good, I'll find someone to cover your class and we can sit down and talk for half an hour or so about what we can do. What period makes most sense for you? Great, bring a page with three or four strategies and I'll do the same. We'll work together to lay out a plan for Peter and Marcus covering from now until the end of the school year. And don't forget to think about how I can support your work. [Principal pulls out her calendar.] Can we get back together in 3 weeks and see how we are doing? OK, you're right, 4 weeks may be better to start. Can you meet on April 27 ? Great, we'll see each other then. And we can also grab each other in the hallway if we have something to share. Or just poke your head in my doorway for a minute. Of course, and I can just poke my head into your classroom too .

The Rolled Sleeve Guideline

Find times and places to get your hands dirty. Roll up your sleeves and join the work every now and then.

Exercise the Broad Shoulder Rule

Develop the habit in public settings of shouldering more than your share of the blame when things go south. Leaders lose credibility and trust when they are seen as throwing colleagues and employees under the bus. They gain credibility and trust when these same people see them as sharing ownership of problems.

Leave Your Ego in the Car

Good leadership is not about you. It is about what you leave behind. When leaders with big egos leave, improvement often walks out the door with them. Good leadership does not depend on personality, certainly not being the big personality in the organization.

Attend to the Curve of Giving

Good organizations develop the habit of providing acknowledgment and rewards to people in the organization. But the curve of giving is skewed upward. Gifts, tangible and intangible, disproportionately follow rank. The people at the bottom of the ladder almost always get less. Great leaders smooth this curve, ensuring that good work routinely done and often unseen is marked by appreciation. They also remember that while honoring a group of workers (e.g., Administrative Professionals' Day) is fine, that recognition tied to specific people and their work is much better.

Keep Flaws in Perspective

Everyone is flawed; some more than others. And, of course, everyone needs to improve. But the world looks quite different when the lens of flaw is privileged over the lens of improvement. Looking for and focusing on areas for development provides a springboard for organizational improvement. Myopic attention to people's faults does not.

Be Slow on the Uptake to Umbrage

Forming umbrage has as much to do with the frames of the leader as the intent of the one "causing" the offense. Good leaders acknowledge this and guard against their own backgrounds and peccadilloes slanting interpretations and judgments. They work to ensure that perceived offenses do not go to seed and thereby promote major problems and incompatibilities.

The Norm of Compounding Foolishness

All people, even leaders, do foolish things. The trick is to learn not to compound foolishness—adding to the deficit through pride and indignation on one hand and hurtful responses to protect oneself on the other hand. Great leaders are adept at taking true measure of themselves and unguarded in their requests for understanding and forgiveness of their foolish actions.

Talk Less

Most leaders talk too much in public meetings—and, for that matter, in private exchanges as well. It is a bad habit that routinely dampens conversation and debate. Practice not saying anything for the first third of meetings. Pick your points of entry carefully.

Reset Personal Exchanges

Personal conversations in organizations tend to center on the leader and their life. There is a convention that because someone is the leader that their vacation, children, hobbies, and so forth should be privileged in conversations. Leaders need to learn to redirect these exchanges. These are the opportunities to learn about the people you work with, not to enlighten them about your life. Used in this manner, these are wonderful opportunities to communicate caring and to help cultivate the trust that is the engine of leadership.

Frame Challenges, Not Problems

Solving problems is a good thing. But meeting challenges is better. The former is often deficit-oriented and tinged with fault-finding. The latter is future-oriented and tinged with a sense of possibility.

Nurture Understanding

Authors over time have provided much guidance that should be honored by leaders. One essential lesson runs as follows: Learn to know what people are thinking about, not what they say .

The Law of the Afterlife

When you die, you are going to the same place as everyone else. There is no special section there for leaders, no matter how famous or effective. Lead with this perspective in mind. You will find yourself being more understanding, generous, and humble. You will find yourself teaching more and telling less. Your business will be better for it. And when you reach the afterlife, you may find yourself being welcomed.

Most Barriers Are Surmountable

In the process of improvement, it is almost inevitable that significant barriers will arise. Ninety-five percent of us arrive at these seemingly insurmountable difficulties, acknowledge the impossibility of further movement, and turn back. Great leaders learn to dig trenches under barriers and find ladders to climb over them.

Structural Changes Do Not Predict Success

Leaders are trained to solve problems and create change by identifying and importing structural changes to the organization. This is problematic. The first iron law of improvement is that structural changes never have and never will predict organizational success.

Let Others Win

Leaders often develop the bad habit of assuming that they need to win every skirmish, debate, point of contention, and so forth—what we call the Ty Cobb Syndrome. It is not necessary and is generally tiresome. Get into the habit of letting others win.

Understand First, Then Judge

Because they are generally in a hurry, leaders often judge a situation before understanding it. Snap assessment and quick judgments are part of the contemporary culture. It is always best to understand first.

The Law of the Dip

Leaders often are an impatient lot. Frequently they hold unrealistic and damaging expectations about the slope of organizational improvement. They expect what almost never happens—a fast start and a rapidly ascending line. As a result, they often damage the very progress they wish to see develop. The great teachers in the domain of change help us see that things almost always trend downward before they begin to rise. This is the period in which high-magnitude mistakes (e.g., withdrawal, scapegoating) are especially apt to occur. Effective leaders understand the law of the dip and manage change accordingly.

Listen—Let People Finish Talking

People often have the opportunity to talk with their boss. Many will also tell you that they were not heard. Take the time to listen to what is being presented. Avoid jumping in with your answers until you take the time to reflect on what each person is telling you.

Learn the Act of Triage

Given the complexity of modern organizations, it is easy to just keep adding material to the importance pile. Yet when everything is important, then nothing is important.

Burn Bridges as You Move Forward

One of the most powerful norms in organizations is regression to the norm. It works like a rubber band, pulling people back to yesterday, old habits, and traditional ways of acting. Leaders gain nothing by denying or railing against this organizational dynamic. It is a powerful force and will continue to flourish long after you have gone. The trick is to be proactive in addressing it, to fight it in ways that can be won. Specifically, leaders must become adept at burning bridges to the past so that backward travel is no longer an option—or, at least, a very unappealing one.

It's Not Personal

A very difficult lesson for leaders to learn—and remember—is that much of the critique that flows their way has little to do with them. It materializes not because of who they are, but because of who they are in the organization. Do not personalize criticism. You will end up being unhappy and dividing people into camps of supporters and nonsupporters.

Err on the Side of Generosity

Organizational life can be tumultuous. Competition is prized. Swagger earned. Sharp elbows, the critical tongue, and the steely glaze are often the norm. Leaders need to understand that this is a precarious platform for either themselves or their companies. Effective leaders—those who make a positive difference and leave something behind—are people who make understanding central to their lives, and who are uncommonly generous to those around them.

Exercise Care in Coming to Judgment

Leaders often make errors when sizing up people. One is the quickness by which they arrive at their assessments. Indeed, many leaders pride themselves for possessing the fast-assessment gene. But leaders are generally better served by a deliberative nature. The patina many people have crafted may be alluring, but it is often fairly thin and forged from base materials. Another is that they provide too much weight to superficial appearance factors, both positive and negative. It really does not matter if someone is dumpy or has a spot on his tie. Leaders form judgments on more important, valid, and reliable criteria.

Don't Let Compliments Die at Your Door

Leaders are uniquely positioned to hear about the successes and contributions of others in the organization. That information is often used to deepen understanding. This is good, but insufficient. Every scrap of good news about employees needs to be passed on—in emails, notes, phone calls, and cards. Remember to attach some of these acknowledgments to concrete expressions of your respect—a book, some flowers, tickets to an event.

Guard Against Unitary Assessments

Leaders often make macro-level or holistic assessments about people who work for them. If someone is good, then that person is good across the board. Or if a person is average, then he or she is average across all aspects of work. This is a bad habit to develop. The world almost never looks this way. Good employees are not usually good at everything. Moving the organization forward depends on the ability of leaders to help people get better in areas in which they are good, and good in areas in which they struggle.

No One Ever Wins an Argument

A little wisdom from Ayn Rand. It doesn't work for parents. It won't work for leaders. Arguments are a colossal waste of everyone's time—and can worsen a situation because they can generally harden positions. Avoid them at all costs.

If Something Is Important to Someone, Then It Is Important (Even if it is of No Importance to You)

Leaders often discount the importance of things—activities, investments of time, material items, and symbols—that are not of particular importance to them. They should know better. If someone cares about something, then it is important. It is as simple as that and you should act accordingly.

Direct the Spotlight of Success Toward Others

It is only natural that when achievements are garnered and successes tallied, leaders wish to receive credit for those accomplishments. It is, however, much more important that others—coworkers and employees—be the ones on center stage as the story of success is told. Learn to deflect credit.

Seek Solutions, Don't Dwell on Problems

One of the major truths of organizations is "that nothing so economizes effort and energy as the knowledge that nothing can be done." And few things lead to the conclusion that nothing can be done more than wallowing in problems. Leaders acknowledge problems, but they move the conversation to the next level. What can we do to solve the problem, get around the problem, or use the problem as a springboard for action?

The Law of the Second Eyeball

The way you see it may not be the way it is. Step back; look again. Get another perspective.

Telling is Not Teaching

There are times to tell. But most times are for teaching. Helping people in the organization learn to learn should occupy a central position in the organizational improvement equation. Telling doesn't carry a leader very far in this direction.

It Is All About the Fingerprints
(And Not Having Your Picture in the Foyer)

Earlier we noted that it is what you leave behind that counts. How do leaders think about impact and legacy? Do you think that when you are dead and gone, to wherever you think you will go, your ghost will return at 5-year intervals to look over the business? The essential question is: Can I see my fingerprints throughout the organization, or will they be quickly wiped away?

Learn to Tell Stories

We live in a world where data are critical and evidence is king. But most of us don't digest information this way. People are moved to action by stories of success. Get into the habit of making your points in this form.

You Can't Buy Back Trust

Trust is the central ingredient in making leaders effective. If people trust the leader, the door to organizational improvement is open. If they do not, it is shut. You should do all in your power to develop it and to defend it from damage. Leadership is a relational idea. Trust is at the heart of those relationships. Once it is lost, it is difficult to impossible to recover.

Be Willing to Abandon Stuff

Organizations accumulate a good deal of organizational sediment over time. One change simply layers on top of the last one. The resulting clutter can choke action. Implementing change requires as much attention to what gets abandoned as to what needs to be added. Learn to jettison.

Wisdom Is Not a By-Product of Promotion

Being promoted does not make you wiser. The possibilities for more intelligent actions that reside in new roles need to be ferreted out and then learned. They don't come with the mantle of position.

Assigning Blame Is Not Productive Work

Things go awry on a regular basis in organizations, sometimes due to forces beyond the control of leaders and sometimes due to human error. When they do, there is a strong inclination among leaders to find someone to blame: "If only Mrs. Jeffries hadn't . . . we wouldn't have this problem." Too regularly, however, once blame is parceled out, the problem is assumed to be solved. The difficulty is that in these cases blaming is a poor substitute for (1) understanding why things unfolded as they did and (2) taking action to ensure better performance in the future.

Shape Ambiguity

All organizations are marked by ambiguity, some a bit more than others. In these situations, people are unclear about meaning. Or they don't know what direction to take. They don't know who to bet on. Effective leaders have an eye open for ambiguity. They understand, often intuitively, that these are places to accelerate progress. People want answers, not more analysis. They want to trust that someone will provide clarity. Leaders seize the opportunity to deepen organizational agendas by fulfilling this need and shaping ambiguity in their favor.

The Law of Replication

When given a blank sheet to work with, almost everyone will draw what they have drawn in the past. Leaders need to provide alternative visions if they expect something different.

Stay Focused on the Big Goals—The Destination

It is exceedingly easy to get pulled down into seemingly meaningful and highly time-consuming activities around the microdimensions of the organization. Details are always important and often require attention. But it is the leader's job to ensure that this work is undertaken in the service of the larger purpose. Without at least one eye on the prize at all times, it is easy for everyone to put in long days and not move the organization any closer to its goals.

Understand the Law of the Pedestal: Expect Attack

Two of the incontrovertible lessons from the study of leadership in the United States are as follows: First, people love to champion and extol leaders; the better the leader, the greater the acclaim and the higher the pedestal. Second, people love to pull their leaders down from these pedestals. It is wise to remember this as you see the pedestal being built. It is simply a matter of time until the same (or a similar) construction crew employs their tools to chip away at the pedestal. It's a cyclical process that in a real sense has little to do with you as the leader. Understand "the law of the pedestal" and you will lead with some sense of equanimity. Fail to understand this reality and you will personalize these actions and likely be much disappointed—and hurt.

Attack Organizational Drift: Take Stock

One of the most profound problems of leaders and the institutions they shepherd is "organizational drift," the tendency to move in a nonplanful manner, incrementally but cumulatively off course. Let's say we start out from Philadelphia, heading to our ultimate destination of Los Angeles. At the end of the first leg of the trip, we are supposed to be in Harrisburg. But in reality, we are 30 miles to the north of Harrisburg. If leaders regularly take stock, we can correct for this drift and re-center the trip. If we don't, we will set out on the second leg of the trip on a straight line 30 miles to the north of where we should be. On subsequent legs of the trip there will be still more drift, sometimes leading back to the original pathways, but often farther and farther away. Instead of ending up in the vicinity of Los Angeles, our organization is likely to end up in Seattle—in other words, doing something it shouldn't be doing. And our leaders will not know why until it is too late to do much about it. Planned stocktaking will go a long way in preventing organizational drift.

Acknowledge the Reality of Organizational Sediment

Remember that the organization was not created the day you were handed the leadership reins. Things build up in organizations—culture, policies, norms, procedures, and so forth. Leaders do not need to be captured by this reality. Yet they need to be aware of it and lead from this knowledge.

Make Feedback Work

Leaders would do well to spend as much time exploring what we know about learning as they do poring over spreadsheets. They would discover that their improvement arc in many areas is steep. One lesson that is a key to organizational improvement merits special attention: using feedback more effectively. Two common errors must be purged. Leaders need to understand that criticism is not an especially helpful form of feedback. It generally does not carry information to help someone move from one point to another. They also need to understand that general praise is not especially useful either. As with criticism, it is devoid of actionable knowledge. Leaders need to provide specific, targeted feedback.

The Law of Boundaries

We have already seen that an essential task of leaders is to create the gravity that holds complex organizations together—and to provide coherence for the organization universe. A related lesson is that leaders need to define the box in which the organizational game unfolds. Degrees of freedom exist inside but not outside the box.

The Law of the Time Clock

No one wants to do meaningless work. Yet much labor in organizations falls into this category. This has nothing to do with the grain size or mundaneness of the tasks and everything to do with leadership. The job of the leader is to ensure that work has meaning.

Do Not Be Led Astray by the Leadership-Management Sophistry

Most of the leadership literature would have you believe that leadership and management are distinct entities, separated by a wide chasm. Leaders are extolled while mere managers are portrayed as competent but poor relations. This is, as anyone who has ever led an organization, baloney of the most misguided variety. Leadership is a simple concept. First, it is about developing a firm understanding of a good place for the organization to be and second, it is about getting everyone to move the institution in that direction. Most of the heavy leadership work unfolds in the hour-by-hour, day-by-day, week-by-week management of the organization. Great leaders almost always lead by managing exceptionally well.

Avoid the Privilege of Allowance

Leaders, especially as they move up the organizational ladder, are often afforded passes of exemption. Because they are deemed important, they can avoid what is expected of others—for example, being on time or doing homework for meetings. Leaders should not ask others to do what they do not.

The Law of Resistance

Leaders need to realize that resistance is normal, often accounting for a significant chunk of the change landscape. If resistance is normal, then people who resist are not pathological, nor are they possessed with major character flaws. Labeling people is not helpful work. Resistance is taught by organizations and learned by employees. Leaders need to see to it that it is unlearned by the organization and its people. Remember that teaching is more than telling.

You Have to Be a Person

Personalized trusting relationships are a key to enhanced organizational performance. In order to have personalized relationships, leaders need to be persons. Great leaders are more than role occupants.

The Art of Seeing the Missing

Good leaders are skilled at seeing pieces of the puzzles. They are adept as well in finding the linkages among the pieces and determining how things cohere. Great leaders also develop the uncanny ability to see what is not there that should be, in discerning the missing. This is a skill set that can be developed, but it must be done consciously.

Don't Alloy Compliments with Qualifiers

A good number of us develop the habit of prefacing or closing compliments with modifiers. Leaders slip into this pattern
as well. "Mark is a bit of a slob, but really a gifted thinker."
"Mary Ann is the best assistant I have ever had, too bad she's
overweight." This is a bad habit to develop. People often walk
away from such exchanges with the modifier in the foreground
and the compliment shadowed. There is no reason for leaders
to engage in this behavior. Find ways to say good things about
people and leave it at that.

Don't Confuse Busyness with Productivity

Most people in leadership positions are exceptionally busy people. They see themselves coming and going, from the first sip
of coffee in the morning until oftentimes well into the evening.
Being busy is a good thing. It provides the avenues for possible
gains. But being busy is never an end. And it sometimes gets in
the way of productivity. To say, "I had a long day and worked
exceedingly hard" always needs to be followed with this codicil:
"And I moved us *several* steps closer to our goal."

The People Who Wrote the Golden Rule
Were Talking to Leaders Too

Throughout the lessons we present in this book a number of
crosscutting themes emerge. One of the most essential of these
is the importance of the human dimension of organizations.
More specifically, these lessons routinely expose the centrality
of relations between leaders and those they serve. At the heart
of the relationship storyline is a simple but powerful leadership
lesson, one that is often difficult to see in action in many organizations: Leaders need to treat all those with whom they work as
they would like to be treated.

Understand the Law of Credit and Blame

The most insightful writers in the area of leadership concluded a long time ago that leaders get much more credit than they deserve when things go well and much more blame than they deserve when things go poorly. As a leader, the law of credit and blame applies to you. Remember to be humble when the laurels are tossed your way. Equally important: Do not be bruised when a healthy helping of blame is served up. And do not accept the mantle of villain too easily.

Everything Done Well

One often develops a sense that in many organizations the big-grain–size activities count a great deal and small-grain–size work matters very little. This is an indication of an unhealthy business, and it exists because leaders permit it. Most of the action in organizations is small-to-mid-grain size work. Each action matters and needs to be done well. Leaders teach people whether this is true or not.

Appreciate the Trip

It is wonderful to reach ambitious goals. But even when this happens, 90% of the action is in the voyage to get there. And in the world of continuous improvement, pulling into the dock is an increasingly infrequent event. Leaders must learn to derive a good deal of their personal satisfaction from shepherding the organization on the trip and watching those around them grow into increasing competence.

The Law of Down

All leaders, from lemonade-stand operators to corporate titans, will be on the mat more than they desire. Leadership shares some of the molecules of gravity. Good leaders understand this reality. They are not disabled by it. Neither do they turn to dysfunctional responses (e.g., justification) to deal with it. They learn to use the down periods as springboards for growth.

Attend to the Slope of Insensitivity

Leadership and sensitivity often move in opposite directions. The higher one climbs the leadership ladder, the easier it is to become insensitive to the feelings of those below, especially those who are two or more rungs removed. There is a natural logic to this, as leaders lose contact with those they lead and reset their sights on higher organizational goals. But the process is not ordained or inevitable. Good leaders are aware of the "slope of insensitivity" and they work hard at remembering that humans are really fairly sensitive creatures. They also work hard to stay in touch with those they lead.

Work Inductively Sometimes: There is Wisdom Down Below

There is a predilection among many leaders to look upward for wisdom—and we might add, outside the organization as well. To be sure, these can be good repositories of knowledge. But as much if not more can be learned, in planful ways, by talking and working with those in the organization, especially those working on the work. As a corollary, it is worth noting that it is the most profound avenue leaders have for teaching.

Test Beliefs

Wise, or at least successful, employees are not in the habit of questioning leaders. Partially because of this reality, leaders develop some bad habits. They mistakenly assume that others agree with them. Worse, they assume that what they believe is right. Both of these states are possibilities, but hardly inevitable. Leaders need to learn to be aggressive in testing their beliefs. If they do not, they will be lulled into zones of comfort that serve neither themselves nor their organizations well.

Keep Values Alive

Beliefs and values are critical components of organizations. Yet in many businesses, they are museum pieces at best and mold-covered oddities at worst. Leaders must be the ones who ensure that important values are nourished. They need to be stewards of organizational beliefs. Others can help haul the freight here, but they need to know what the load is that they are being asked to carry.

Use the Law of Equifinality Well

Although less emphasized than in decades past, the Law of Equifinality remains robust. That is, there are usually multiple ways to reach desired ends. Good leaders know this. They do not, therefore, misspend precious resource and energy dragging employees back to the one true pathway, which is almost always theirs. They use this law to build ownership in the work and commitment to the organization. Because of this, they gain a good deal more than the single prize at the end of the trip.

Not All Help Is Helpful

Well-intentioned assistance needs to be provided artfully, that is, with an eye on the perspective of the person being helped. What seems to you as helpful action on your part might be seen as an indicator of failure on the part of others. Assistance not carefully planned can kill initiative and nurture dependence. Display some caution before jumping in to solve the problems of others. Nurture the art of getting invited to assist. Learn to teach others to succeed rather than to hand out solutions.

Open Leadership Is Better Than Closed Leadership

Transparency is a popular concept. But it is often honored more in the breach than in reality by leaders. Leadership by secrecy is no more effective than leadership by intimidation. It does not foster the development of productive relationships nor nurture the emergence of trust, which is at the heart of all leadership. It creates skepticism and promotes the formation of cliques. Being too open can sometimes get a leader in trouble; but that is always a better kind of trouble than that which comes from secrecy.

Reposition the Lens

Learn to look through the eyes of those around you, those who work for you in particular. We each create and polish lenses based on an assortment of factors, gender, age, and so forth. Seeing how others view the world in general and the tasks at hand empowers leaders. It is a piece of the "care" narrative reported above. And it is an essential component in the understanding gene that powers great leadership.

Confront Problems Directly

In many businesses, we find leaders who approach problematic behavior in an odd manner. Rather than confront the source of the problem directly, they communicate (generally by email) with everyone in the unit, shop, or division. This may make life easier for the leader, but it almost never has an impact on the person who needs to hear the message. And it angers the rest of the people who are already playing by the rules. This is a weak piece of leadership.

Deprivatize Practice

Letting and encouraging good people to head off and work alone feels right. Generally, it isn't. Removing bureaucratic barriers is wise. Letting employees become isolated is not. Effective leaders understand the power of collective learning. They carefully orchestrate work so that it occurs.

Run Two Engines

Freud listed two elements of a meaningful life: love and productive work. Turning to leadership, we alter that formula a bit to include hard work and intelligence. There are important messages for leaders here. First, hard work is wonderful, but when it is decoupled from intelligence, it is a much less powerful tool. Second, intelligence is wonderful too, but no leader should think that they have a Get Out of Hard Work Card.

The Law of Double

Mark what you think can be done. Double it. You will not likely reach the target.

But you are apt to blow by your initial markers of success.

Leadership Has Its Own Vices

There are a number of garments that leaders often accrue as they climb the organizational ladder. Self-importance, arrogance, blindness, disrespect, and similar outfits are increasingly found in leaders' closets. Particularly damaging is the sense of entitlement with which leaders often cloak themselves. They come to believe that they are permitted to operate differently from those who work for them, that leadership provides a warrant for special treatment. Many leaders have discovered that this is an especially slippery slope on which to stand. It is never a mechanism for building a strong organization. It is sometimes a pathway to self-implosion for the leader.

Play at the Edge

Think of the organization as a circle, with safety in the middle and risk taking on the outer surface. Almost all the pressures from inside and outside the organization push leaders to the center of the circle. The problem with this is that it is almost never the place where new ideas, proactive endeavors, and entrepreneurial actions are found. Average leaders stay in this low productivity comfort zone. Good leaders play at the outer edge of the circle, with one foot inside and one foot outside. If you have both feet out, you will be killed off as a radical. With both feet inside, you'll end up as a caretaker. Good leaders know, often intuitively, that they need to have one foot in and one foot out. They also know that it is good to be a small irritant at times.

Beware the Binder

Organizations are notorious for developing thick binders of information that are expected to direct actions. They are full of information such as policies, contracts, operating procedures, and so forth. Binders have their place in running the organization. They just don't have much to do with leadership. "Managing through the binder" may keep you out of trouble, but it is not likely to make you an effective leader nor help you build a highly effective organization.

Monitor What Is Important

There is a prevailing adage in the leadership world that what gets monitored gets done. The advanced version holds that what gets monitored and informed by that action gets done. Leaders often assume that things are getting done and being done well. Good leaders, on the other hand, are aggressive monitors. They have a set of three to five critical issues that are never far from their minds and hearts as they run their organizations. In addition, they watch the organization all the time through a "monitoring monocle." They know there is a difference between looking and seeing.

Learn Lessons of Failure and Loss

A good number of initiatives come to less-than-desired ends in organizations. No one wins all the time. And failure is never on vacation. All of this is normal. What is not routine is the planful use of these results in the improvement process. No one likes to poke at wounds. Indeed, leaders are quick to haul mistakes off to the landfill, often throwing blamed workers on the trash heap as well. But effective leaders understand that the strategy provides false comfort. They work hard to make failures and losses into platforms for learning. In so doing, they fortify foundational pillars such as risk-taking and innovativeness.

These and Those People

Good leaders know that there are no "these people" and "those people" in the organization. They understand that these labels are crutches for weak analysis and impediments to organizational effectiveness.

Context Always Matters

No two organizations are the same. No two employees are the same. No two problems or opportunities are the same. Knowing standard ways of doing business is important. But good leaders never lose sight of the second iron law of improvement: Context is always important. For leaders to be effective, this means following one of two paths. First, always pick situations that align with the way you lead. Second, learn to adapt the way you lead to the prevailing context—culture, life cycle of an intervention, organizational history, needs of employers, and so forth. Since the first pathway is often not an option, wise leaders become adept at understanding organizational context and tuning their leadership accordingly.

Avoid the Allure of "Rightness"

Getting the organization to where it needs to be is more important than you being right. There is no need to bludgeon employees with reminders of your brilliance. It sends an assortment of nonhelpful messages and dampens enthusiasm for investing energy in the next organizational journey.

It Is a Small World (Disney Was Right)

It really is a small world. Many people are going to recycle through your life at unexpected intervals. Leaders who are generous, especially in victory, and who use defeat as a springboard for improvement rather than a rationale for retaliation will be enriched by these reconnections. Leaders who do not will carry damaging baggage into these renewed encounters.

Hire Brighter People Than Yourself

Leaders are sometimes (often) gun-shy about surrounding themselves with people more gifted than they are. This is a profound leadership error. It says much about a leader's self-confidence. Good leaders understand that they are only as good as those who work for them. They also know that organizational quality will always shine on them.

Learn to Manage Up

Leaders often assume that their job is to take the rules of the game and the materials that are handed them and then set out on the leadership voyage. This is a critical part of the leadership narrative, for sure. But to be most effective, leaders need to understand they can manage up to shape the rules of the game and determine the tools they are provided. Leaders must be proactive in shaping the expectations and systems that expand or confine their leadership.

Values Are Essential

Data and leadership have always traveled well together. Indeed, data are essential to making good decisions. Values and leadership have traditionally enjoyed a less healthy relationship. Indeed, much work over the years has been devoted to forging out the impurities of values in the making of leaders. But values are a critical component of effective leadership, both for determining the ends that are selected and in choosing the processes used to reach those goals. Leaders need to take time to understand and assess their values. And they need to work on supplementing their portfolios when they discern missing or poorly developed values.

Honor the Law of Attention

Strong leaders make those with whom they interact feel important. They are particularly adept at this art in their interpersonal relations with employees. They do not convey distraction. Nor do they look over people's shoulders when talking, scanning the room for "more important" people who need their attention. When exchanges occur, others believe that they are at the center of the organizational universe. They leave with a sense of specialness and often enhanced commitment.

Explain *No*

While it is an admirable practice for leaders to routinely find their way to *yes, no* is an organizational reality. Less effective leaders often justify *no* with references to organizational rules, procedures, budget constraints, and so forth. In the process, they also often damp down creativity and initiative. The best leaders learn to explain *no* in terms of the organization's mission. In so doing, they are more likely than their colleagues to invite employees to continue their investments in the business, not to pull back to their cubicles and just do their job. *No* needs to empower people, not stunt their commitment.

The Mirror of Guile

Many leaders develop a belief that people who "look" like them—who resemble and reflect their characteristics—are most effective. The reality is that people can be annoyingly different and also very effective. Good leaders avoid the seductive trap of expecting everyone to follow the paths that they have walked.

Remember the Denominator

Many leaders have been led astray by the allure of the numerator. Individual numbers become decontextualized, assuming greater meaning than they should. To be most effective, leaders need to remember that it is their connection to the denominator that provides importance to the numbers above the line.

Mentor All the Time

Good leaders are strong mentors. They consciously work to help others learn the art, craft, and science of leading. It is part of the DNA of good leaders, not simply a set of actions they turn on when someone is assigned to them as a mentee. Good leaders keep their eyes open all the time for opportunities to impart the lessons of leadership. And because these messages may not be intuitively obvious, they take the time to explain the moves they make.

Actions Rule

Modeling through actions is by far the most powerful way for managers to lead and to convey the underlying values of the organization. Leaders can write until their fingers fall off. They can talk until their tongues fall out. But they need to remember that what they do will most influence people.

The Deceit of Universal Goodness

Leadership pushes people toward the assumption of universal goodness. If you are good, then you are good at everything. After all, you are the leader. This misconception ossifies as leaders climb the organizational ladder. It is often fueled by those above and below, and by the vanity that increases as each rung is mastered. Great leaders understand the guile of this assessment, especially as it applies to them. They are adept stock-takers of strengths and areas for development. As a consequence, they manage more effectively than their myopic counterparts.

The Law of Carving Stew

Organizations rarely mirror the tidy entities that most of us prefer. They are more like a stew than a meat-and-potatoes meal. What does this tell leaders? First, different ingredients can work equally well. And they generally can be mixed in varying amounts and still produce a quite satisfactory outcome. Recipes can help, but they can only carry a leader so far. Second, the almost maniacal need that leaders have to chunk up the organization should be tempered somewhat. You cannot carve stew.

Confront Problems

Organizational scholars and leadership analysts help us see a key difference between less and more effective leaders. When troubles come, poor leaders allow their organizations to focus on responses that confound those troubles: avoidance, withdrawal, blaming, denial, reinterpreting the problem, defending the current state of affairs, providing justification for the failure, and concealing the trouble. Good leaders force themselves and their colleagues to confront problems.

Examine Yourself

The advice has been around from the time of the ancient Greek philosophers. It applies to us all. But it has special significance for leaders. It is not difficult for leaders to end up becoming people that they don't know—and that others don't recognize either. It doesn't happen overnight. It is a slow, steady, and, often after a certain point, inexorable process. Leaders lose sight of who they are and what they stand for. The only way to address this tendency to drift is to routinely examine one's own leadership. Avoid the inclination to justify actions and explain away problems. Develop a critical lens. Commit to 10 minutes of reflection every night on the way home. Use a common protocol each time. Put what you learn into play in your organization.

Geography Cannot Save People

There is a widespread belief that change is good for people, especially those who have been less than successful elsewhere. Good leaders know better. Troubles in one place almost always tag along as a person heads to a new position. What is required is learning new ways of being and doing. Geography by itself cannot accomplish this.

The Future Is Ahead

Traveling backwards rarely carries an organization into the future. While re-centering action around touchstone values is always advisable, perseverating over an unalterable past action almost never is. Forensics is not without value, but rarely so when decoupled with strategizing the future.

Readiness for Not Acting

Leaders by definition and lore are actors. They often assume the swashbuckling persona, cutting their way relentlessly to the prize. This action role can be addictive, however; assuming independent life and becoming decoupled from your organization's mission. The most effective leaders are on their guard here. Strong actors, for sure. But they also nurture the patience and wisdom required not to act.

Follow Your Own Sermons

Few things damage leaders more than their failure to follow their own advice, and to adhere to the values they espouse. Because this is a universal truth, effective leaders have learned to be parsimonious in promulgating advice. And once advanced, they are religious in adhering to their own preaching.

Caring Counts a Lot

Leaders who use others as ends will almost never be as successful as those who promote an ethic of care in the organization. People work hard for leaders they respect. And they are more likely to respect leaders who care about them as workers and people and who create an organization that embodies that sense of care.

Create Your Own Future: Be Proactive

Many leaders find themselves thrown into the river of management and frequently directed by the tides and eddies they encounter. Good leaders take charge of their work and their careers. They take the time to determine where the organization needs to be and how they propose to get there. They experience the same turbulence and buffeting as do other leaders, but they don't let it control them.

Simple Kindness Works Best

Leaders are often portrayed as the steely-eyed dispensers of justice. People who err on the side of toughness, handing out rewards to the few and disapproval to the masses. Leaders often bend to fit these portrayals. When they do, they make a great mistake. Effective leaders know that what people deserve is kindness. Thoughtfulness extended is generally reciprocated with trust. And trust provides much of the scaffolding that allows leaders to do their work effectively.

There Is Always a Back Door

It is easy to develop a singular focus of coming in the front door on problems, challenges, and development work. When the door is locked, leaders pound harder. When that proves inadequate, they try to break the door down. Successful leaders have learned that there are almost always other ways into issues. They do not continue doing the unsuccessful over and over again out of stubbornness or a need to show people that they are the boss. They walk around problems until they find a side or back door, doors which are often already open, or at least unlocked.

Honor the 95-5 Rule

Highly effective leaders think a good deal more than they talk. Something in the neighborhood of 95% investment in learning and 5% of talking seems right for leaders.

Lead from the Center

Organizational charts always show leaders at the top of the food chain. Sometimes it is a big food chain; for example, a regional office or division. Sometimes it is a smaller food chain, like a single store. But the top-of-the-chain logic is always the same. Leaders generally are taught and therefore operate as if this is the best way to think about leadership. Good leaders know better. The best leaders understand that they need to lead from the center of a web—a web of relationships, not a chain of authority. In this model they know that their actions produce much deeper effects as they spread outward. They know that this is a much more effective way to get things accomplished than trying to have things cascade down the organizational chart.

Don't Be a Martyr #1: Remember Your Family

When all is said and done and you are not leading the organization anymore, you'll still have a spouse and children. It would be nice if they were still in your life and they still knew you. This will not be the case if you become a martyr for the organization. There are indeed times when nearly 100% of your energy will need to be invested in the organization. But if this becomes the norm, you will likely pay a heavy price for it on the family front.

Pouting and Whining Don't Work

These strategies don't work well for children. They do not become more viable because one is a leader. Leaders do not have the option of picking up their marbles and going home. Nor do they enjoy the luxury of holding grudges. You will be defined in part by how you deal with adversity. Grace and renewed commitment go a long way here.

Understand Collaboration

Leaders—poor, average, and great—have taught us a good deal about meaningful collaboration and how to nurture it in an organization. They have shown us that it is easy to be hoodwinked by poor substitutes: acceptance of the least robust point of agreement, dictated consensus, and going along with the most aggressive and noisy. They help us see that collaboration is a shared process for elevating solution strategies.

Remember the Power of the 3 x 5 Card

Three-by-five cards do not carry much cachet in the high-tech world of today's organizations. But they can be quite helpful for leaders. First, leaders need to put what the organization is all about and where it is headed on one of these cards. Second, they need to get in the habit of handing out these cards to a good number of the people they run up against.

The Law of Unpacking

Good leaders are often unaware that they need to pull apart their effectiveness for others, especially less-seasoned colleagues. These leaders have collapsed a great deal of knowledge and wisdom into forms that are fairly dense and, therefore, not intuitive to others. These nonexperts struggle to replicate the leader's expertise, and often fail in doing so. Great leaders need to become adept at unpacking the density of their knowledge base, showing it to others in pieces and steps. Planful explanations and deliberate modeling are preferred tools.

It Is Better to Direct than Star in the Production

Contrary to popular belief and prevailing myths, good leaders are more concerned with getting the organizational stage set and helping others act well than they are with being the central protagonist of the story. To be sure, success is dependent on the leader. But when the question is asked, "How were we able to be successful?" you want the recognition and acclaim to be distributed widely throughout the organization, not directed primarily at you.

The Truth About Armor

Here is what we know about personal armor. First, almost everyone grows some. People damaged in life and at work grow more. Second, armor generally finds expression in ways that are off-putting, sometimes passively, often actively in the form of less-than-helpful interpersonal actions. But here is the lesson that great leaders have learned: Kindness melts armor. And once this happens the formerly armored become a leader's most steadfast and ferocious defenders.

You Can't Bury Mistakes

In the face of nearly universal evidence that it does not work, many leaders act as if they can undo mistakes, missteps, and errors of judgment by denying them, throwing up smoke screens, or burying them. Evidence consistently confirms the futility of these cherished strategies. They almost never work. And they generally compound the initial mistake. This is the case because the following observation nearly rises to the level of a law in organizations: Bodies don't stay buried. Leaders need to develop the courage to accept their mistakes. It will always be a lot less painful than other strategies.

It Is What You Leave Behind That Counts

Most of us do not think about it that often, but we will all leave the unit or system we are leading. The question of how things look now is not unimportant. But more important questions are: What is the legacy of leadership? How will the organization look in 5 to 10 years? Have the valued elements become deeply ingrained? For too many leaders, the good they created walks out the door when they leave. Good leaders focus on deep change. They leave the organization permanently improved.

Past Is Prelude

Another law of improvement is that the best predictor of future performance is past performance. The leadership lessons here for managers are abundantly clear. Two stand out. Surround yourself with successful people. Allocate work to those with a track record of success.

Mistakes Can Be Illuminating

Leaders, like all humans, make mistakes. Many leaders, however, compound these missteps. They act as if mistakes are not normal. They treat mistakes as things to be explained away or buried. Good leaders see mistakes differently. While not condoning repeated errors, they clearly understand that mistakes can teach one a great deal. They see missteps as learning opportunities, pathways to improvement. Poor leaders learn nothing from their own errors or the missteps of others—and they fail to help others learn from their mistakes.

Prevention of Problems Trumps Remediation of Problems

Throughout the preceding pages, we have touched on three of the iron laws of improvement that provide powerful lessons for leaders—structural change does not equate with performance, context is always important, and past is prelude. Here we introduce the fourth law: Prevention of problems is always a wiser strategy than dealing with them when they emerge. And the corollary is that early intervention always trumps later intervention. Good leaders don't put off tough decisions until a crisis is at hand.

Don't Be a Martyr #2: Develop a Personal Brake

Running until one implodes is not a good way to lead. Leaders need to develop a personal brake and they need to learn how and when to use it. Without this tool and knowledge, one of two things often happens: The leader burns out, in which case they are of little use to the organization. Or the leader begins to resent this personal sacrifice—and takes it out on the very people they are supposed to be helping reach important goals. Developing a sense of balance is essential for leaders.

Don't Hold Grudges

Developing a grudge in response to some insult or slight may give the leader some satisfaction in the short run. But it will get in the way of moving the organization forward. Grudges are toxic to the process of getting work done. They convey a less-than-desirable message to everyone else in the organization. Because reaching goals trumps feelings, leaders need to be extraordinarily generous in overlooking and forgiving actual or perceived insults.

You Can Do Without Cynicism

Cynicism often comes off playing well in the movies and novels. It is a poor ingredient in the leadership stew, however. It almost always damages rather than helps people lead. It carries the seed of inaction, often destruction. It provides a platform on which little or nothing can be accomplished. It may be cute, but it's not leadership.

Practice Saying *Yes*

Over time most leaders develop a strong propensity to say *no*. Overwhelmed with input and subject to what appear to be constraints on every front—resources, policies, contracts, culture, history, and so forth—*no* becomes a central word in the vocabulary of leaders. It is also quite often the most cautious and safest response. Leaders can get into trouble much more quickly when they take actions than when they allow the status quo to run its course. But leaders in high-functioning organizations are adept at finding their way to *yes*. They understand that it is usually only through new actions and efforts that programs can be achieved. Keep a list of the requests that come your way. Don't begin with *no*. Tell people you need to mull things over and that you will get back to them. Work to see why opening doors trumps closing them.

Internalize the 30% Vision Rule

I run up against leaders all the time who are just beside them-selves that people haven't internalized organizational mission, goals, and direction. They are simply perplexed that information that was written down and talked about at various meetings has not penetrated very deeply. My colleagues need to remember the "30% vision rule": When the leader is so tired of hearing about and seeing the mission and goals that they want to jump overboard, then that is the point where about 30% of the orga-nization is familiar with them. Connections to the other 70% should lie ahead—not critiques of their obtuseness. You cannot overcommunicate about goals. They need to be talked about all the time. They need to be in almost every written communica-tion. They need to be item number one on every agenda. And they need to be visible everywhere in the organization.

Avoid the Allure of Agreeableness
(or Keep Your Adversaries on Your Hip)

It is only human nature to wish to consort with those who like you, agree with your opinions, and support your plans—and ac-tually enjoy your company. Leaders are not exempt from the pull of this gravitational force. But they need to guard against "the allure of agreeableness." Good leaders make conscious ef-forts to check regularly with those who usually do not agree with them—the critics, the skeptics, and the unhappy. Leaders who don't end up with a really skewed understanding of their organizations.

Forgiveness Starts at the Top

Leaders need to understand that leading is not simply managing a procession of the happy and contented. And they need to understand that the unhappy and malcontented have a habit of saying not-nice things about and doing not-nice things to leaders. Quite often, these are hurtful actions. Not surprisingly, they often have the intended effect. But leaders are in no position to dwell on these injuries. Good leaders are slow to internalize and quick to forgive.

Write It, But Don't Send It

Always avoid immediate responses to troubling emails. If you don't, you generally will wish that you had. You cannot withdraw e-mails. If you need a cathartic experience, reply but do not send your response. Sleep on it. You will find yourself deleting almost all of these responses the next morning.

Capture Short-Term Wins

Chroniclers who cobble together narratives of strong leaders help us see that they are masters of beginning with the end in mind, that they are tenaciously clear about desired goals and assiduous in planning to achieve those objectives. But they also illuminate another theme. Effective leaders are also masters at "chucking" work into manageable units so that ongoing victories are secured. They are especially adept at this during the early stages of the voyage. They accumulate short-term wins to undermine skepticism and doubt, and to nurture a sense of possibility. They don't simply ask everyone to engage for the long haul and await the time when the final prize is secured. They actively structure short-term accomplishments.

You Can't Say Thank-You Enough

Good leaders are aggressive about introducing acknowledgments into the system. They faithfully adhere to the following rule: You can't say thank-you enough. And they have a plan of action to bring the rule to life. Thank-you notes must fly off the desk of the leader—and not all emails. Letters of commendation for quality work and extra commitment should flow to personnel files. Tokens of gratitude should regularly appear on desks. Posters and banners acknowledging the leader's appreciation for hard work and success should line the halls. Plates of cookies and fruits with thank-you notes should be ubiquitous. Personal statements of thanks should be part of almost all conversations and laced through every meeting. The rule is to express appreciation as often as possible in as many ways as possible and to be specific about the content of the acknowledgment.

Food Opens Doors: Bring Candy, Fruit, and Cookies

There are few universals in the leadership guidebook, but this is one: Food smoothes the pathway of leadership. It sends an important message: that you care about people, which, as we reported in an earlier lesson, is another proven pathway to leadership success.

Don't Take Yourself Too Seriously

If you are not careful, you will find yourself in the same boat with colleagues who share an overinflated sense of their own importance. Those who work around you can often feel this. It is not a solid platform for leadership. Remember that you are important, but not that important. And remember that importance has more to do with what you do for others than who you are. Try not to take yourself too seriously. And help others on your team follow the same advice.

The Good Leader's Mantra: Focus, Focus, Focus

Analysts who study leaders and leaders themselves tell us that their lives are marked by an incredible amount of variety. Fragmentation of effort is the norm. The DNA of interactions is brevity. They are pulled and pushed hither and thither in all directions attending to a never-ending stream of highly diverse responsibilities. The problem here is that it is common in this environment for leaders to lose connection to the centrality of mission and purpose. On the other hand, good leaders are remarkably adept at holding the rudder straight in these choppy waters. They rarely lose sight of the destination. They adhere to one of the critical guidelines of improvement: Focus, focus, focus.

The Work Is Its Own Reward

Acknowledgment of one's work is always nice. Recognition is appreciated as well. Yet effective leaders understand and act as if the reward is to be found in the work itself, not in the emoluments that accompany the work. It is from doing the work well that they draw their sense of success.

Adhere to the Principle of Building Up

If you study leaders for any time—those in business, historical figures, managers in the nonprofit sector, and so forth—you will see many managers who act as if the climb up the leadership ladder is made possible by tearing others down. You should avoid this pitfall. Effective leaders get ahead through their own efforts and on their own merits, not by running down colleagues and supervisors. Work well done provides much better footing for leadership than does bad-mouthing others.

Start as Well as Put Out Fires

Leaders are, for good reasons, characterized as firefighters. They are portrayed as running around, often frenetically, putting out fires in their organizations. They are also taught to believe that when all the fires are extinguished and calmness prevails, the business is in good order. This is an error. Effective leaders are as adept at starting fires (e.g., creating a sense of urgency for needed action) and managing fires (e.g., keeping initiatives in play) as they are in putting out fires (e.g., squelching a problem).

Focus on *Cans*

As we noted earlier, one of the great laws of organizations is that nothing so economizes effort and energy as the knowledge that nothing can be done. If it cannot be done, then there is little reason to marshal energy, time, and related resources in the service of organizational goals and objectives. Focusing on why things *cannot* be accomplished is a crippling impediment to leadership, both in terms of establishing meaningful ends and for getting people to move toward those ends. Effective leaders search for the *cans*.

Enjoy the Work

When I was a young leader, I had a colleague who saw the world through the lens of retirement. The really good stuff in life would begin when the job ended. My colleague died 3 years before he was set to retire. A tragedy for certain. But not one without a valuable lesson. The prize isn't out in some distant future. It needs to be garnered day by day, month by month, and year by year. All of the truly fine leaders whom I have known over the years have reinforced this powerful lesson.

Develop a Good Understanding of Consensus

Almost all the leaders whom I have worked with have a very poor understanding of consensus. The nearly universal position is that consensus means everyone. This is profoundly wrong. Consensus is almost always some portion of the whole, not the entirety. There are three ingredients that go into the consensus mix, and they shift in weight depending on the situation: percentage of people, presence of key leaders, and depth of feeling. In some cases, if all the leaders thought of as critical in a business are on board, you can have consensus even if the majority does not support a certain direction or strategy. In other areas, 80% support may not be consensus if there is vehement opposition and key leaders are not on board. Good leaders do not equate consensus with unanimity. They are adept at reading the three critical elements.

Assume Little

When I was a young leader, I entertained a group of employees representing their colleagues who saw a problem and offered up a solution. Everything they said seemed reasonable and action steps were put in place to address their concern. A week later, I was skewered by the balance of the employees. My mistake: assuming that this small cluster of employees actually spoke for their colleagues—and that their desired solution was widely shared. An important lesson was etched into my rules-of-action guidebook: Assume little, check everything. Good leaders honor this principle in their work.

Be Persistent

Most work is hard; it isn't a smooth walk downhill. It is almost always a truism that people will get tired, grumpy, dispirited, and worse on the voyage—much of which is uphill and on crooked pathways. There will be points where it is clear to many if not most of the travelers that success is highly unlikely and that the trip should be suspended. It is at this point that most leaders stop. Highly effective leaders push on. They know that often-times the only thing that distinguishes success from failure is persistence.

Follow the Goldilocks Principle

I hear all the time that leaders need to have a thick skin, they can't let things affect them. And I have worked with and studied more than my fair share of leaders who adhere to this maxim. The problem is that it is not accurate. Leaders can't wear their hearts and feelings on their sleeves. They cannot be so thin-skinned that they are pushed and pulled hither and thither. But having a heavily lacquered veneer hurts leaders more than it helps. Leaders need understanding. While some of that wisdom comes via the head, much comes from empathy, the ability and willingness to feel what touches others. This doesn't occur for leaders with thick skins.

Leaders Are Teachers

All leaders teach all the time. Every act sends a message. Leaders teach by how they spend their time and with whom—and how they talk with others. Everything matters—where they park their cars, how they dress, how they do (or don't) invite participation in meetings. Good leaders know this and are proactive in their exercise of this responsibility. Not-so-effective leaders seem oblivious to this reality. As a consequence, they fail to capitalize on all varieties of ways to help others grow and develop. Even worse, they often convey messages that they wouldn't if they knew better.

You Can't Do It Alone

Many leaders make a fundamental mistake early in their careers, and they have a devil of a time undoing it: They confuse being in charge with doing all the work. It is, as most leaders learn, an especially wobbly and unsustainable leadership platform. Leaders who stand on this stage are rarely successful, or successful for any sustainable length of time. Good leaders diffuse responsibility throughout the organization. They learn that it takes many pairs of hands to do the heavy lifting of organizational improvement.

It Is Not About Charisma

The leadership literature, and much of the apparatus in the workplace, perpetuates the ideal of the charismatic leader—charming, highly visible, full of dash, always on point, and somewhat noisy (in a nice way). Many act as if this is the correct frame of action for leaders, the larger-than-life head of ship. It isn't. There is nothing wrong with being charismatic, but most good leaders are not. Most are simply quietly effective.

Ask Questions All the Time

Good organizations are complex, rapidly shifting enterprises. They are characterized by the need for a plethora of solutions to constantly surfacing problems. Because of this reality, leaders often assume the mantle of "answer person," dispensers of solutions to all manner of organizational conundrums and personal problems. Some of this is appropriate and helpful. But too much is actually harmful. Leaders need to be equally comfortable wearing the mantle of "question person." Or, more eloquently, leadership is about a pedagogy of questions. It is only in this manner that leaders provide the guidance required to help others learn how to attack problems productively. It also helps leaders remember that they don't know everything.

Protect Those Who Follow Your Leadership

As we reported earlier, leadership is a marvelously simple concept: Find a good place for the organization to travel to and get people on board for the trip, which also includes getting them to undertake the work in making the trip successful. This means that good leaders have lots of people following them, many walking with them hip to hip . Good leaders do not forget this. They are fiercely loyal, albeit not blindly so, to those who put themselves out for the good of the business. But many other leaders are more than happy to throw team members under the bus when problems surface, accusations fly, and the clamor for accountability reaches a crescendo. In the process, they send all the wrong messages through the organization.

Beware the 100% Rule of Success

Leaders often rejoice when 100% of the people reach 100% of their goals—100% of the time. Failure has been conditioned out of the system. Unfortunately, when the potential for failure walks out the door, it takes risk taking, innovation, and proactiveness with it. Good leaders understand that when the 100% Rule of Success is in play it is distinctly possible that little is actually being accomplished. These leaders do not expect people to hit all their targets. What they expect is for people to set ambitious goals and move close to achieving them.

Changing the Organizational Chart Does Not Change the Organization

It is almost axiomatic that leaders begin by changing the organizational structure of the business. Some roles are combined. Others are moved. Still others are eliminated. New reporting relationships are firmed up. A new logic is imposed. All very tidy indeed. The problem here, as good leaders know either intuitively or from experience, is that such changes have almost no impact on organizational effectiveness. In reality, it is the most feeble type of leadership.

Play to Your Strengths

Leaders have two core pathways to follow in leading and in becoming better leaders. They can identify areas of weakness and labor to improve skills in those domains. Or they can deepen areas of strength. Almost everyone tells leaders that they should follow the first avenue. This is not inappropriate. And it can lead to enhanced leadership skills. On the other hand, this guidance did not come down the mountain with Moses. Many leaders would be better served to deepen areas of strength. A balance between the two designs is needed. But most leaders are not in balance here. And effective leaders always play to their strengths.

Survey Well First

In many businesses, people end up doing the wrong work, in the wrong way, with the wrong tools. This is almost always a failure of leadership. Huge amounts of capital go into all sorts of poorly planned work. Worse, in many cases it isn't even the right domain of work. It is as if the workers are 2,000 feet down in a coal shaft that need not have been drilled. Busyness overrides questions of effectiveness. Good leaders are first and foremost master surveyors. They always spend the time getting the drilling site correct before they get people engaged in work.

Leaders Are Learners

Great leaders are defined by their positive stance toward learning. First, such a perspective reminds them as well as everyone around them that they don't know everything. When leaders act as if they do, they only get into trouble. Second, it conveys the message that learning for everyone is important. And where leaders fail to convey this message forcefully through their own actions, they ensure that organizations never reach their full potential.

Light Can Blind as Well as Illuminate

A good number of workers labor in a narrow rut with a very limited field of vision. Many leaders understand that if real achievements are to be gained, those people need to be brought out of the rut. They need to develop broader perspectives and new ways of doing business. Too many leaders fail to understand, however, that this process is as likely to blind people as it is to help them see newly illuminated possibilities. Leaders then become perplexed (and worse) when these people do not see what is perfectly visible to the leader. More effective leaders understand the powerful and positive consequences of bringing people into a new world of knowledge, work, and possibilities. They ensure that the transition is gradually and successfully completed one step at a time.

Create Gravity

Organizations by design splinter. Old pieces become isolated, disconnected. New pieces are often poorly hinged to the body of the business. The good of the whole gives way to the benefit of the unit. Great organizations are coherent systems that work in harmony. This does not occur by accident. It happens because good leaders consciously attend to it. Indeed, perhaps the most crucial role of the leader is to create a center of gravity that holds the organization together. Great leaders know this. And they continually add implements to the toolbox that they employ in undertaking this critical work.

Install an Off Switch

For all leaders, there are people, usually colleagues, who cause their "engage and fight" switch to clink on. There is nothing wrong with leaders flipping on this lever. The problem is in letting others have access to the switch. When others do the turning, the exchanges are rarely productive. Time and energy are usually squandered, progress halted. Worse, others gain even more control over the switch. Good leaders know how to control the switch to "engage and fight."

Learn to Appreciate Messiness

Leaders often top the list of people who enjoy closure, getting things boxed up and squared away. And often with good reason. But leaders need to know that insight and creativity often develop in messy and cluttered environments. Good leaders understand that it is better to have clutter than to have things squared away for the sake of order and neatness. They learn to expand their scope of tolerance for ambiguity as well.

The Rationale Crutch

It is normal to explain away unwanted effects. "A competitor received the contract because it was wired, the company had insiders in the game." "A colleague received a promotion because she was annoyingly cloying." Normal behavior, yes, but unproductive for the leader and their company. Yes, impacts have many roots, some less worthy than others. But a focus on rationales limits learning—and demeans others. Good leaders have the toughness to get beyond rationales, to unpack the real reasons behind effects. They seek understanding.

The Equation Error

An easy mistake for leaders to make is to assume that opportunities and requests from above have more meaning or value than those from below—or from oneself. If the opportunity originates two or three levels up, then it is even more meaningful. By definition, requests from above are important. But importance and meaningful are not synonyms. Good leaders learn to apply the test of meaningfulness, as well as importance, to work.

It Is About Service, Not Power

I've had more than a few colleagues over the years who let their leadership appointments go to their heads. (See the earlier lesson on Leaving the Ego in the Car.) Worse, they came to believe that leadership was about power, getting to throw their weight around, if you will. Power is an important element in the leadership algorithm, but it is not the central variable. Good leaders understand that leadership is more about service to the community in behalf of reaching valued ends than it is about power.

The Law of Failure

There is no firewall between you and those who work for you. When your people fail, you fail. Their failure is your failure.

Change Is Not Improvement

Perhaps the most critical error that leaders make is to equate change with improvement. Most leaders learn this inaccuracy as they move up the management food chain. Things are better here because we have a new _____. Things are better here because we changed the way _____. Things are better because we saw what _____ was doing and we copied it. Change is the sine qua non of many organizations and leaders. The problem is that there is not a strong connection between change and improvement. Good leaders know that change efforts are important, but they are never ends.

Perception Is Reality

Leaders often live in a tightly defined, rational world. To an important degree, this is good. But there is more to organizations than rationality. Politics and feelings come to mind, for example. A critical ingredient here is people's perceptions. Leaders often engage in efforts to "change" perceptions without ever understanding them and without recognizing a core condition of life: Perceptions are reality. And there is a corollary here too: Direct attacks or showing people that their perceptions are wrong—usually with an assortment of data—are not especially effective.

Optimism Is Essential

There are a number of essential traits or characteristics that are linked to successful leaders. Earlier we discussed persistence and consistency. Here we introduce another essential characteristic: optimism. Work in organizations is often difficult. The pathways to success are often poorly charted. If located, they are found to be inadequately marked. And they are generally rocky and often covered with brush. The trip in turn is often arduous, and success can be elusive. Pessimism can become a constant traveling companion. The single person best in position to keep spirits from flagging and commitment high is the leader. They need to convey an aura of possibility, a sense of hope. They need to be constantly upbeat about what can be accomplished. In short, they need to be unabashedly optimistic about the future—for today, for tomorrow, and for the long haul.

Honor Disagreements

It is generally pleasant to be around people who agree with you. Most leaders build their organizations accordingly. Dissension is suppressed. So too oftentimes are innovation and progress. As annoying as it can be, the best leaders know that they are more likely to learn from those who disagree with them. Equally important, they honor this truth by creating an environment where differences are legitimized.

Beware the Silver Bullet

Many leaders are in constant quest for the silver bullet of improvement. They believe in the big event that will carry them and their organization to the top of the mountain. Good leaders have learned otherwise. There is no magic lantern, holy grail, or silver bullet in the improvement chronicle. Good leaders understand that each well-developed intervention, program, initiative, and so forth, will add only a small measure to the success storyline. It is the ability of leaders to bring a collection of these small gains to the table that defines a good system. And to foreshadow the future, they remember the Principle of Integration as they engage in this work.

People Only Speak for Themselves

Leaders need to learn that most of the time when colleagues say that they are speaking for someone else, they probably aren't. Or at least they may be putting a spin on an idea or feeling that the person being spoken for might not recognize. Don't accept "speak-fors" as accurate. Always follow up personally with the person represented.

There Are No Secrets in Organizations

The following types of comments are often heard in the conversations of leaders: "Keep this one between us." "Don't let this go any further." "Keep this under wraps." "Don't let this one get out." "No one is supposed to know about this so keep it to yourself." What leaders need to learn is that almost nothing stays under wraps. It is simply a matter of time before what is supposed to be secret is widely known throughout the organization. If you want something to remain private, keep it to yourself.

Remember the Law of Negative Transfer (or All Negatives Come Home to Roost)

We just argued that leaders need to learn that there are no secrets in organizations, everything becomes public. The only unknown is how much time the process will take. The corollary to the lesson of secrecy is the Law of Negative Transfer: All indirect negative comments you make as a leader will find their way back to the person or persons who are the object of those remarks. It is inevitable. The wise leader will learn to scrupulously avoid conversations and public pronouncements in which criticisms of third parties are made or implied.

Make Your Boss Look Good

In an earlier lesson, we suggested that leaders should become adept at deflecting credit outward to those who work for them. Here we provide a related lesson: Good leaders are strategic in ensuring that their bosses get a good deal of notice when things go well. The adjunct is that they need to be careful not to dump on the organization when things go awry, even when such critiques are warranted.

Guard Against the Allure of Omniscience

It is easy for leaders to fall into the trap of assuming that they know everything. Even when they don't enter this trap with alacrity (which they often do), they are often pushed into this position by nearly everyone with whom they work, both inside and outside the business. Leaders assume the mantle of omniscience at great peril, however. Good leaders become adept at saying: "I do not have an answer for that one at my fingertips. Let me look into it and get back up with you by _____."

Teach, Don't Do

Leaders have a tendency to want to jump in and solve problems for others when they arise. All the forces in the organization reinforce this proclivity. Good leaders resist these forces. They learn that their role is to help others solve problems. They know that success with the problem must rest with the person, not the leader. Good leaders teach the tools of problem-solving and provide needed supports. They don't take ownership of the problem from the learner.

Passion Matters

We have argued that bosses need to develop the traits that define great leaders. We spoke earlier about the importance of persistence and consistency and about the power of optimism. Here we note that passion is at the heart of all good leadership. Great leaders exhibit a deeper and more intense emotional drive about their organization than do normal leaders. They believe in what the organization does and that what the organization does matters.

Learn the Principle of Integration (or More Stuff Does Not Mean More Success)

Many leaders believe that the amount of stuff going on is related to success. The portfolio of stuff becomes a marker for effectiveness. Good leaders, on the other hand, have internalized the Principle of Integration. That is, while getting goods in the portfolio is important, the key work is forging coherence and alignment among programs, interventions, and strategies. Integration of the stuff is essential for success.

Don't Wound Your Enemies

It is not uncommon for leaders to encounter people in the organization, who for all manner of reasons, are bound and determined to undermine their leadership. Elsewhere, we suggested that ignoring these individuals is not a wise idea. Here we add that wounding them is even worse. They will only become more ferocious adversaries and more tenacious in their oppositionality. They may lie low or go underground, but they don't go away. There are only two productive ways to engage this organizational reality. One, you can work with them to get them onto the team. Two, you can remove them from the organization. There are places for kindness and consideration in the leadership equation, but this is not it.

Problems Don't Disappear

Leaders often delay dealing with problems that need attention. This is a serious mistake. Problems fester. They become bigger. They infect other dimensions of the organization. They harden, becoming less malleable to action. Good leaders have learned that it is almost always better to address problems than to wait and hope that they will go away on their own.

Employ a Two-Fisted Approach to Improvement

All organizations have two essential components—a core technology or production system and a culture. One of the most powerful leadership lessons from the research on organizational improvement is as follows: Leaders need to work on both dimensions of the organization to garner maximum gains. Work on either one alone will be much less effective.

Rules Change: Learn to Be Flexible

Leaders spend a good deal of time building systems and structures. Getting things fixed into place is important. On the other hand, organizations shift around a good deal. People come and go. Procedures and systems evolve or get scrapped. Rules change. There is a tendency among leaders, however, to hang onto old ways of doing business, or at least to complain regularly about new ways of doing things: "Who in their right mind thought this up?" "What could they possibly be thinking?" Good leaders on the other hand are fairly nimble. They understand the importance of flexibility. They know that game changes are part of organizations. They spend much less time bemoaning change and much more time helping their businesses make essential moves to meet shifting internal and external environments.

Learn to Use What You Already Have Better
(or Learn to Look in the Cupboard First)

Some leaders are regularly looking for something new to solve their problems: a new program, a new strategy, a new intervention. Good leaders look for new programs too. But they are also much more attentive to and much more adept at using what they already have more productively. They are masters at combining existing assets in new ways. The leadership lesson is to always begin by examining existing resources.

Know the People You Lead

Throughout these lessons we have argued that leadership is fundamentally a matter of relationships. It is difficult to lead people that you do not know. Good leaders know (and care) about the people in the organization. They understand what motivates colleagues as well as their hopes and concerns. And they devote the time required to develop that knowledge.

Don't Confuse Excuses and Explanations

In some organizations, explanations for troubles and other shortcomings often take the form of excuses. Good leaders understand that excuses explain away the need for renewed action. They work diligently to uncover reasons for less-than-hoped-for progress, but they do not allow these reasons to become barriers to renewing the struggle for the prize. They are good at organizational forensics. But while many of their colleagues see this as the endgame, good leaders use explanations as a platform for further organizational growth.

Humor Counts

Earlier we reported that food is a universal lubricant. Humor is another. It helps keep organizations running. And it keeps leaders from taking themselves too seriously.

You Can't Teach Wisdom

Good leaders understand that wisdom emerges from experience and reflection. It can't be imparted directly. Colleagues must grow into it. Effective leaders know that they need to spend a good deal of time setting the organizational stage and arranging the props therein so that wisdom has a chance to develop.

Remember to Tell People What You Did

A week does not go by when I do not run up against a leader who is disgruntled because the good work they have done on behalf of someone has gone unrecognized. Oftentimes when we drill into the matter we discover that these are not, as presumed, cases of insensitivity or absence of gratitude. What we discover is that the leader's work is completely unknown to the other person. Good leaders are adept at closing the loop here. They not only get issues taken care of, but they also make it a rule to get back to the person whom they are working for and let them know what was accomplished and why. Communication really is the wonder drug of organizations.

Critique in Private

If you have a criticism to deliver, do it in private. And don't offer it in a roundabout manner.

You Gain Power by Giving It Away

This is a difficult lesson for leaders to learn and an even more difficult lesson to practice. Many leaders adhere to the vault model of power, the belief that there is a fixed amount of power and that the wise thing to do is accumulate it centrally and spend it as you need things. Good leaders act differently. They understand that capacity and capital can much more effectively be created by empowering others.

Maintain a Horizon Perspective

One of the most powerful lessons my mentors have taught me over the years is that the best leaders keep their eyes on the horizon—and the best of them can see over the horizon. They are routinely scanning to see what the future is likely to bring so that they can build on, overcome, or adapt to these realities. By attending to this scanning work, they become pretty good at seeing the future. In many situations in which I've been involved, the leaders were so busy watching current operations that they allowed the organization to be run over by the future. The lesson is straightforward: Keep an eye on the horizon.

Anticipate Negative Consequences

Most leaders are pretty good at getting their heads around the good stuff that they expect will accompany new policies, programs, strategies, interventions, and so forth. The best leaders, however, are also effective in discerning what negative baggage is likely to hop a ride on the new program train. Since it is a thousand times preferable to deal with potential negative consequences before they materialize than after they appear, the leadership lesson is as follows: Always think through the negative—as well as the positive—potential consequences of proposed changes.

Remember the Three-Dimensional Law of Attack

Strong leaders understand that to successfully move an organization they need a battle plan that emphasizes three lines of attack. They understand that they need to use the power at the top of the organization and have it cascade downward. They know they must engage in a lateral manner. And they realize that they need to push upward from the bottom. Any individual line of attack is likely to be ineffective. But good leaders have learned that magic can happen when they engage all three.

Success Is Fragile

Good leaders know this to be true and act accordingly. They have learned that success is more like a flower than a building. It requires regular attention, and they ensure that it is provided. Many other leaders have never learned this lesson. And they are routinely frustrated when hard-earned gains vanish.

Mark Success by How Much You Accomplish on the Bad Days

Benchmark against what you are able to accomplish on the really tough days, when everything seems to push you away from your objectives and plans. If you can do well here, you will almost inevitably do well overall.

Everyone Starts with a Clean Slate

Many leaders who enter new situations fall into the trap of forming judgments about people based on old evidence and second-hand reports from their predecessors. Good leaders start with the assumption of competence and commitment. People are given the chance to demonstrate whether the assumption holds. They may end up earning an exit ticket from the bus, but they are not denied a seat at the start because of the previous leader's opinion.

Learn to Complain Appropriately

If I could have a dollar for every time I have been in a conversation with a leader who is complaining about something to people who have absolutely no ability to address the complaint, I would be wealthy. Some of this is cathartic and of no harm. But a good deal of it actually damages the fabric of the organization. It infests the culture—and the Law of Negative Transfer tells us that these complaints will wind their way through the organization. Leaders need to learn that complaints must be directed to people who not only listen, but can also address the problem.

Flush Out Slackers (or Don't Battle Underground)

In many organizations there is ample room for uninvested and unproductive people to hide. Actually, we often create hiding places for these people. The best leaders are moved to address this problem. But they have learned that it is much easier to engage the matter when these people are pulled out of their burrows and exposed to the glare of colleagues and stakeholders.

Don't Be Too Liberal with Advice

There is a fine line between providing advice and condescending, a line defined by the person on the receiving end and not the leader. Many leaders are somewhat obtuse in this regard. Good leaders read the advice narrative more accurately. To begin with, they realize that such a line exists, and they are careful in the distribution of advice. Second, as discussed above, they learn to lead through questions as much as answers.

Imprint the Law of Continuous Improvement

Leaders need to practice their craft from the knowledge that the organization should never really reach its end. More importantly, they need to teach others that the business is continuous improvement. Key milestones are definitely reached. But new ones are established simultaneously.

Pressure and Support Work Best Together

So far, we have laid out a number of leadership lessons that emanate from work on effective organizations (e.g., work in three directions at once; employ a two-fisted fight on improvement). Here we add an additional lesson: Leaders must learn concomitantly to apply pressure on the organization to change and provide needed supports. Focusing on either element alone will not be nearly as effective.

Remember the Law of Bi-Directionality (or There Is No Steady State)

Leaders need to understand that there is no status quo when it comes to performance. Your business is either going forward or backward. When talk turns to maintaining ground already captured, you are headed in reverse.

Nurture Patience

We have already introduced most of the critical traits that leaders need to develop: passion, consistency, persistence, integrity, flexibility, and optimism. Here we add a seventh: patience. It is difficult for experts in most fields to remember what it was like to be a novice. It is oftentimes difficult for people who know what needs to be done—and how and why and when—to let other people develop that understanding as well. But good leaders separate from the norm here. They know that they will not always be there to tell people what they need to do. They lead with the knowledge that others need to own issues and develop ways to tackle those issues. This requires patience in abundance at times. Good leaders keep a lot of it in the bank.

When You Leave, Go

The literature on effective leadership is thick in many areas, but thin in others. Observation helps fill some of these gaps. One of these lessons is that highly productive leaders display an uncanny sense of timing and grace in respect to their own careers. They know when it is time to hand over the business to others. They also have the wisdom to know that when they depart, they should not take up a position on the periphery of the stage. When they leave, they go.

About the Author

Joseph F. Murphy is the Frank W. Mayborn Chair of Education at Peabody College of Education at Vanderbilt University. He is the coauthor of *Positive School Leadership: Building Capacity and Strengthening Relationships.*